Fossils

LEVEL 11

DECODABLES BY jump!

Teaching Tips

Lime Level 11

This book focuses on developing reading independence, fluency, and comprehension.

Before Reading

- Ask readers what they think the book will be about based on the title. Have them support their answer.

Read the Book

- Encourage readers to read silently on their own.
- As readers encounter unfamiliar words, ask them to look for context clues to see if they can figure out what the words mean. Encourage them to locate boldfaced words in the glossary and ask questions to clarify the meaning of new vocabulary.
- Allow readers time to absorb the text and think about each chapter.
- Ask readers to write down any questions they have about the book's content.

After Reading

- Ask readers to summarize the book.
- Encourage them to point out anything they did not understand and ask questions.
- Ask readers to review the questions on page 23. Have them go back through the book to find answers. Have them write their answers on a separate sheet of paper.

This edition is published by arrangement with Booklife Publishing.

5357 Penn Avenue South
Minneapolis, MN 55419
www.jumplibrary.com

Decodables by Jump! are published by Jump! Library.

Library of Congress Cataloging-in-Publication Data is available at www.loc.gov or upon request from the publisher.

ISBN: 979-8-88996-945-7 (hardcover)
ISBN: 979-8-88996-946-4 (paperback)
ISBN: 979-8-88996-947-1 (ebook)

Photo Credits

Images are courtesy of Shutterstock.com. With thanks to Getty Images, Thinkstock Photo and iStockphoto. Cover – Mark Brandon. 4–5 – Babyboom, AkemiO. 6–7 – liga_sveta, imageBROKER.com. 8–9 – Esteban De Armas, adike, Natalia van D. 10–11 – Microgen, VectorMine. 12–13 – MarmadukePercy, Bjoern Wylezich, Michael Rosskothen. 14–15 – Galyna Andrushko, Bjoern Wylezich. 16–17 – FunkMonk, Alex Coan. 18–19 – Hohum, Zack Frank. 20–21 – BabichAndrew, WH_Pics.

Table of Contents

What Are Fossils?

The ground under our feet is full of secrets about life on Earth. Among the rocks and soil, fossils can be found. Fossils are shapes in rocks or the ground that have been left behind after a plant or animal died long, long ago.

Some fossils show us parts of animals that lived millions of years ago. When a part of the body of a plant or animal is left behind, it is called a body fossil. Footprints, eggshells, and nests can be left behind too. These are called trace fossils. These tell us how an animal lived.

How Fossils Form

Normally, when a plant or animal dies, its body rots away into the earth. But sometimes, the body might be covered in sand, mud, or ash from a volcano. When this happens, the soft parts still rot, but the hard parts are protected. Slowly, they are smashed and squeezed into a fossil.

When a fossil forms, it is called fossilization. Over time, rock forms in and around the body until eventually there is only rock left behind in the shape the body once was. A fossil is not made of the creature itself. It is more like a rocky statue made inside a **mold** of the body.

Under the Sea

Many fossils form under the sea. The **seabed** is the perfect place for fossilization to happen. When sea creatures die, many of them sink to the ocean floor. The sand on the bottom of the ocean is always moving. It buries the bodies before they can rot away.

Ammonite fossils

An ammonite may have looked like this.

Earth's surface is always moving too. An area that was once at the bottom of the sea might eventually end up somewhere very unexpected. Sea fossils have been found at the tops of mountains and in other areas nowhere near the sea. Fossils tell us about animals. They also tell us about the history of the planet itself.

Dig Back in Time

By digging down into the ground, scientists can see back in time. The farther down through the layers of Earth we dig, the further back in time we can see. Scientists use the different layers of rock and the fossils they find to make a timeline of life on Earth.

This timeline is called the **geological** time scale, or GTS. The GTS breaks the history of Earth into different time periods. These time periods tell us what animals were around at that time. The first dinosaurs lived in the Triassic Period around 250 million years ago.

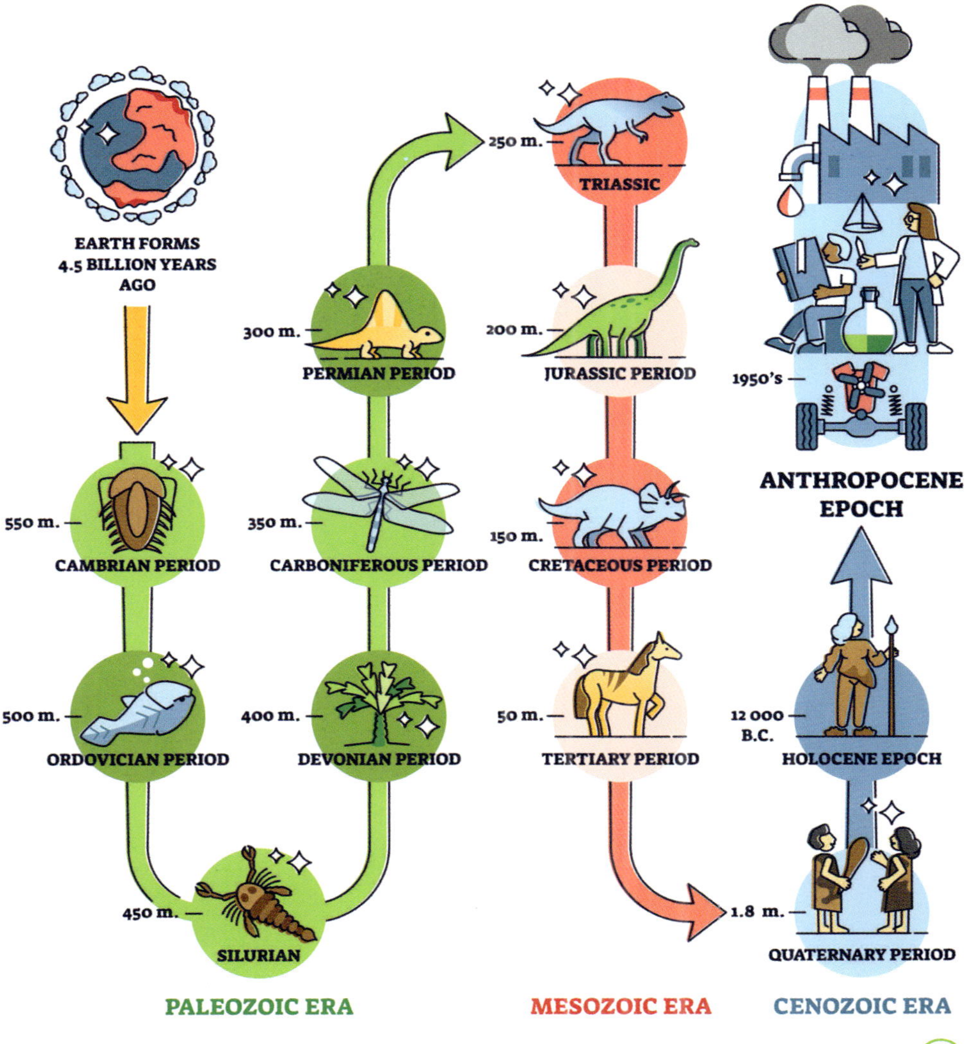

Big Bones

In 1676, a large bone was found in Oxfordshire in England. The bone was given to a man called Robert Plot. No one had heard of dinosaurs back then. Robert Plot thought the bone came from the leg of a giant person! Now we know the bone came from a dinosaur called Megalosaurus.

Robert Plot

Another Megalosaurus bone was found around 1820 by William Buckland. He was the first person to guess that this bone came from a huge lizard. Around the same time, Mary Anning discovered many fossils on the beach at Lyme Regis. They turned out to be Ichthyosaurus, which means "fish lizard."

In 1841, Richard Owen named these strange, **ancient** beasts "dinosaurs." This means "terrible lizards."

Amber

Not all fossils are found in rocks. Sometimes creatures get stuck in a thick, golden liquid that comes from trees and plants. If the creature is completely covered, the animal can be **preserved** exactly as it was when it got stuck. Over millions of years, the liquid hardens and becomes solid. It is called amber.

Insects in amber

Often, small animals and insects are found in amber. Sometimes, pieces of larger animals have been found in amber. Unlike fossils, amber preserves the animal just as it was. Some real animal bones can be found in amber!

A tiny frog preserved in amber

Prehistoric Poo

Coprolite is a very famous type of fossil. A coprolite is fossilized animal poo! This means it is a trace fossil. Coprolites come in all shapes and sizes, from less than one inch to more than 26 inches long! Coprolites can tell us a lot about what dinosaurs and other animals ate.

Different types of dinosaur poo

If we know what creature left the coprolite, we can figure out whether it was a meat-eating carnivore, a plant-eating herbivore, or an omnivore that ate plants and meat. If we know what is in the coprolite, we might be able to figure out what left it! Scientists compare coprolites to modern animal poo.

Fossilized shark poo

Finding Fossils

People who look for and study fossils are called paleontologists. Mary Anning was one of the first paleontologists. She learned to hunt for fossils with her father. They called the fossils "curiosities." Mary found a 17-foot-long skeleton when she was only 12 years old! She became known as one of the greatest fossil hunters.

Some places have so many fossils they become famous. The Jiufotang Formation in China is a famous fossil site. It is around 120 million years old! Many fossils have been found in the Hell Creek Formation in the United States. It is the only place where Tyrannosaurus rex fossils have been found.

Hell Creek Formation

Famous Fossils

Lucy is a fossil of an early human **ancestor**. This means she can show us what humans used to be like. Lucy lived more than three million years ago. This makes her one of the oldest human fossils ever found. Almost half of her full skeleton has been found.

Lucy

Sophie is the most complete and well-looked-after Stegosaurus skeleton ever found. She is 9.5 feet tall and 18 feet long. Sophie lived around 150 million years ago, but the fossils were not found until 2003. Sophie is on display in the Natural History Museum in London, England.

Sophie the Stegosaurus

Index

How to Use an Index

An index helps us find information in a book. Each word has a set of page numbers. These page numbers are where you can find information about that word.

Page numbers

Example: balloons 5, 8–10, 19

Important word

This means page 8, page 10, and all the pages in between. Here, it means pages 8, 9, and 10.

Questions

1. What did Robert Plot think the big Megalosaurus bone was?

2. What is a coprolite?

3. What is Mary Anning known for?

4. Using the Table of Contents, can you find which page you can read about fossils forming under the sea?

5. Using the Index, can you find a page in the book about amber?

6. Using the Glossary, can you define what a seabed is?

Glossary

ancestor:
A member of a family who lived long ago.

ancient:
From a period long ago.

geological:
Relating to the study of Earth's structure, including its rock layers.

mold:
A container with a certain shape that people pour liquid into so that it sets in that shape.

preserved:
Protected so that it stays in its original state.

seabed:
The floor of the ocean or sea.